# THE CHAIN

## A GRANDMOTHER'S REFLECTIONS

# The Chain
## A Grandmother's Reflections

# Poems by Valerie Taylor

# *Dedication*

To My Daughter

## *Synopsis*

THE CHAIN IS A SERIES of poems about the experience of becoming a grandmother.

Valerie Taylor charts the narrative from the moment her daughter announces her pregnancy to the birth of a second daughter. The title reflects the concept of a chain through the female line of a family and their links through genetics, emotions and unconscious movements and shifts - how they manifest through Valerie's observations.

On hearing of the first pregnancy, Valerie remembers in a poem, her own first moments of pregnancy with her daughter. Through a series of poems she reflects on different feelings she experiences on the approach of the birth.

The poems then move through the early weeks of the new baby's life, indirectly referring to the often difficult period of adjustment. There follow poems which show the deepening bond growing between mother and baby daughter, then a connection between grandmother and granddaughter - the first smile. Different facets of this new role, where the grandmother is close but outside the initial family group, are explored and illuminated and offered up for reflection.

The grandmother experiences joy, awe, self-doubt, awakening of old memories and wonders about unconscious genetic links which pass down through the chain. There are generational differences, struggles, discoveries and greater self-knowledge created through this journey.

The narrative arc culminates in the birth of a second granddaughter when the grandmother is able to slide into her role with more ease. Valerie acknowledges then, the importance of her daughter and finally reaches a point of reparation in her role of a grandmother, significant to her unique circumstances.

Every grandmother, (and grandfather) has different situations but many of the feelings and experiences described here will be universal.

# Contents

**The Chain**

## *The Chain*

The chain of mothers stand
back into the centuries;
memorial ghosts,
leaving their silent templates,
each woman painting her own version
in a subtly different style.

## Crossing the Line

'I'm pregnant Mum,'
her voice falters.
I can hear her waiting
for my response.

Thirty years gather up,
heave back like a wave,
and we are two frames
superimposed on a Kodak roll,
alchemy of features and curves,
light fusing and blurring.

On a hot July night, then,
I dreamt of my new baby,
that I was accused
by Mrs Thatcher's government
of contributing to the
population crisis.
He saw it first, the brown ring.
heavy, thick. Dark crystals.

Suddenly I'm breaking inside.
Breathless. Paralysed,
unable to move forward,
stunned at something
so normal happening to me,
after years of imprisoned fertility.
He wants to tell everyone.
I want to hold it to me,
ease myself into the new shape.

It's stamped hard into my memory,
even that faint whiff of
myself before motherhood;
I crossed a line to
a life unknown
in the rented flat
in South East London,
cat litter on the floor,
books in piles,
sun in the garden.

'I'm pregnant, Mum,'
her voice filters
through my bones,
rearranging my feeling of home.
I hug her slight hesitation,
flooding it with my own joy
moving it from between us.

## *Growing*

We drink tea in a flat in Peckham.
My daughter is heavy, anchored
by the weight of the baby.

It's still and hot.
An occasional slither
of cool air
exhales through the skylight.

What will I leave her
from my inheritance
as she awaits her motherhood?

A line is now drawn in the sand.
I see my mother's spiral of anxiety
visible within me; I am
battling to break the mould,

working in quiet therapy rooms
staring at my reflection,
trying to understand

unconscious messages,
mysterious familial patterns
which transfer in flesh and breath,
leaking through, despite intellect,
intention or desire to control.

Gifts of my life's wisdom
bestowed over this cup of tea
are brushed away.

Without articulation,
my daughter conveys
that her path belongs to her.
It is not mine.

I have not quite
seen that I have my own.

## *Waiting*

The shadow of the house lies
across the moonlit fields.
In the quiet deep of night,
my nerves shrill, lungs clutch air;
waiting at the window,
waiting at the brink.

She once lived within me,
the ghost of the umbilical chord
still in my subterranean world,
braided to her, even though
the fleshly knot is gone.

I wait at the window.
She waits for her baby
to struggle across
the line of entry and exit
to leave her safe sleepy world.

And she at the brink
of ragged transformation,
about to lose the independent
young woman she was,
in the solitary battle
to become a mother.

Suddenly, at this
breath starved moment,
clogged with feeling,
do I see that my own
giving birth was traumatic
and has leaked up into
my eyes, thirty years later,
from the delicate casket buried
inside me from so long ago
where lies my jewel,
my baby, my daughter,

remaining like a template
carved into my papery memory.

## *Circle of Light*

What can I do, poised
on the periphery of this event?
Waiting...picturing them
Father, Mother, Baby...
perhaps I can surround them
in a circle of light?
Will this make them safe?

In a city of
a million psyches
trapped in flats;
their partitioned rooms
beneath criss-crossing
silvery vapours of planes,
there will be a moment
when the signal goes
and the baby
begins her journey.

The breathless hours will
send her in stops and starts
as she is pushed
down the warm canal
into a strangely lit room,
faces gazing down at her,
as she is placed in
the open arms of her parents.

She will lie on her mother.
Skin on skin;
her parents' tones and smells
as familiar as the dark place she lived in,
where their voices echoed
in her watery world.

She will feel the rhythms of their breath
and burrow in the milky folds,
rocking and murmuring
in her mother's arms;
always wrapped tightly,
as eventually she begins
to open her eyes
and distinguish the map
of their faces, their smiles,
sensed before through muted sounds
she has heard in her safe dark sleep.

As I await my granddaughter,
above us all in the frosty night sky,
lies the illuminated stitching
of Cassiopeia
anchored on starry infinity.
The constellation - complicated and minute
to the human eye.

It's all I can do,
keep picturing them
in a circle of light.

# *Mirror Image*

In the silence of
frost and stars,
the sky is a cathedral
arching up to
pin-pricks of light;

layers of gossamer
veils in black folds,
mapped with sharper,
brighter luminescence.

The mystery of
her arrival hides
in the galaxies,

a shiver of light
arcs across the sky,
streaks amongst stars
to the clear horizon.

A shooting-star moment
in her brain triggers the chain,
firing off the synapses,
beginning the journey
from her own tender
tight universe, close
to the gentle rhythms of
the protecting, beating heart
as she separates, arrives,
and rests in her mother's arms.

## *The Birth*

I dress in lamplight,
movement slowed by panic;
scarcely taking sufficient breath,
I carry my bags downstairs.

Dawn lifts November light,
cold breath of coming winter;
cows motionless in the gloom -
their eyes following me
from room to room, as
I gather what I need for my journey.

I drive into the bitter air,
trees burnished in their mineral sheen;
sky heavy, disturbed, bruised;
shot with veins of early sunlight:

speeding up wet roads,
which stretch, like
shining grey ribbons
across Salisbury Plain.
I'm on a silver stream,
flying across the hills;
luminescent, now
dented with shadows,

to hold my daughter,
see the face of her baby,
who shifts us along the line,
her mother in the middle,
grandmother at the edge,

as she arrives in
the fragile radiance of Autumn.

# *Arrival*

Near Stonehenge, I check my phone.
Talk of 'helping the baby out.'
'She is tired. So tired.'

I drive down roads I've known
for twenty years of my life -
suddenly there are one-way systems,
blocks, dead ends, roadworks.
And no parking spaces.

Round and round
the streets of Camberwell
in an existential no-man's land
circling the hospital where I want to be,
losing my special moment with her.

In the lift, I am hot, breathless,
hair wet with perspiration;
through swing doors, which will not open
without numbers punched on a pad.

Behind the blue curtains my daughter
on a high bed, tired, smiling,

holding this new person.

In my imagination, I believe
I can see in the baby's sleeping face,
the woman she will become.

## *Comfort  Blanket*

She's here.
brutally extracted
from her dark safety.

The mild gingery Autumn
into which she was born,
is suddenly consumed
by a storm of wild white snow.

It drifts in ghostly flakes
over the city, silently covering roads
roofs, trees - softening their edges;

layers transform into a frozen shield,
an icy surface on a once alive world,
so delicately exposed,
as the temperatures shrink
deeper and winds form soft mountains,
harbouring her, protecting her.

She lies swaddled,
her raw warm life,
wrapped tightly
in a lacy shawl.

In the flurries cascading from the sky
are memories of the stars
where I searched
for the mystery of her birth.

The wind drifts
the glinting snowflakes
up their front door,
blinding the air outside to
the sound of the baby's husky cries.

## *The Call*

Snow falls in November.
Words on the radio stir up fear.
'Icy'. 'Treacherous.' 'Blizzards.'
'Do not travel unless your journey
is absolutely necessary.'

Her voice on the phone!
She needs me to come.
In the car, I plunge into bitter air.
Blindly. Mindlessly.

White flurries feather from the grey weight of sky.
Her distress drives me through bitter air;
my car and I are alone,
speeding along tracks left by earlier journeys.
Her words lodge in my stomach.
I push on through the blizzard.
'Hog's Back' is voluptuous in snow.
Hard, dark branches of trees
disappear into white flourishes.

Mid-afternoon and I reach Kingston,
the loneliest part of the journey over.
Only an hour away, the worst done.
I'm amongst houses now,
safer and warmer.
There's movement and people.

## *The City*

In the London dusk,
cars are stationary,
red lights,
eyes of rooted animals,
beside, ahead, behind,
exhausts exhale
frozen breath,
silhouettes of drivers motionless.

My sense of achievement dissolves;
I'm trapped in a long-standing present.
The vision of her at the door
vanished, future ceased.
I crawl, a segment in a caterpillar.

Traffic lights flicker through their
illuminated sequence, fruitlessly.
Teenagers walk home from school,
in dark coats, hurl snowballs at friends.
Houses dead and cold,
with dark, vacant windows.

The gloomy light of day,

shrinks to night,

hours marked by radio news,

I cling to her voice on my mobile.

A policeman, rubbing his hands,

bends to the window and directs me

to another queue of cars, inching forward.


Late at night, exhausted, anxious,

I begin to recognise the geography

of houses, shops, roads.

Snow, brushed aside by wheels,

lies heaped in gutters,

pale crystals hover and fly in lamplight.


The door opens;

she's holding the baby,

they're haloed in electric light.


There is pie and mashed potatoes in the oven.

## *Staying*

Night turns the day over
like a page. My daughter
is exhausted from her broken sleep.
I am drained by the journey.
We sit, side by side on the settee in silence.

I make tea and toast.
Hold the sleeping baby,
while my daughter showers.

Snow rests on the branches of
the ginkgo tree in the garden.
The transport system has seized;
voices on the television talk of
'horrendous weather conditions;'
Passengers at airports appear static;
helpless; surrounded by bags.
Limbs break on ice; queues appear in A and E.

Then we escape the airless central heating,
walking in freezing slush,
the baby clasped tightly in her arms.
We are silent, our cheeks flushed with cold.
The baby cries and the cranial osteopath
lies her on the couch, gently touching her head.
She is still.

## *Three of Us and Baby*

Three of us in that snowbound flat
move around silently, while the baby
in her post natal discomfort,
cries and cries, the television drones
in the background; in the stillness,
heat and absence of a future,
each of us awkwardly struggle
to manoeuvre ourselves into
new roles, assigned by
the arrival of this baby.

This primitive maternal force
drove me into possible danger,
so urgent was it to keep my promise
to myself, to be there in those
hard times in the early days
of mother and baby's struggles
to harmonise their pairing.

Yet how much could
I have worried
those who loved me,
impelled as I was
to rush into the snowstorm;
my need to protect, driven by
the power of the genetic chain.

Now, I realise that I must soon return,
driving in horrendous conditions,
squeezing myself into a moment between
one danger and another, without knowing
which is the safest choice.

Alone on the pump up bed,
I lie sightless in the dark room,
while the couple sit together,
discussing their nightly tasks;
who will walk the baby.

### *H o m e*

A bright crystalline day -
a sign for me to leave;
to sever the cord.

I drive through cold slush,
mud splashing across my vision,
the windscreen liquid freezes;
sun glances at an angle,
firing into my eyes,
a visionary blast from the sky,
blinding me;
cars scream past as, heart thumping,
I crawl into a garage for safety.

Salisbury Plain is a different blindness.
Night layers upon fog, hedges and fields vanish
in a thick opaque mass, creeping around me.
I hear metal of cars, smashing in my brain
as I struggle to follow the red lights ahead,
star-burst reflections streaming across sore eyes.

At night,
swamped in the duvet and
dreams of my daughter,
I long to soothe the shock
of her seismic shift
from woman to mother.

In my arms is a visceral memory
of the baby's curved back,
legs folded close to her,
soft snuffly breath against my neck.
She is not here, yet she is -
twinned with my daughter
when she was a baby,
their weight feeling
so similar against my body.

In the morning
cold dawn light lifts
the winter sky.

Our future begins...

# *H e l p l e s s*

The baby's husky cries drift on the wind,
rain struggles at the window panes,
as the storm surges around the empty house.

She floats through my dreams,
catches me in the almost-waking
edge between dark and light;
hovers in my senses,
nestles in my imagination.

I feel her solid shape
under my palms and fingers,
in the circular web of my arms;
the weight of her trust,
her cloudy breathing - somnolent,
as if still living in the womb,

blind to outside life;
as am I,
with helpless adoration.

## *She Emerges*

In the weeks which follow,
I drive from Devon to London,
while my daughter, pale,
sits, rooted to the settee,
holding the baby, who cries,
sleeps, sucks her hands and
feeds with desperate fervour.

I walk her up and down the corridor,
trying to rock her discomfort away.
She seems to inhabit a secret underworld
which we have all forgotten.
As her weight becomes heavy,
I, too, sit on the settee, watching
the ginkgo tree in the garden
begin to bud, as I realise
I could never have told
my daughter that it would be like this,
just as no one told me. I had forgotten.
A mother sometimes needs to forget.
Besides, for her it may have been different.

Then Spring lightens their rooms.
The buds on the ginkgo become leaves
and the baby's body grows solid and strong.
She learns to bounce in her mother's arms,
thrilled at herself, she shrieks and screams.
A frown appears when she concentrates, urging
to discern, perceive or understand
a change of tone, or two voices exchanging.

She converses, gazing at her mother
making repetitive noises, grasping at vowels,
imitating language shapes and cadences.
Her almond shaped eyes are alive, dark, intense
with laughter, intention, humour.
She gives the signal with a sound.
And awaits her answer.

One day our eyes touch and there's a smile.
Her face is alight, as is my heart.
She and I go back and forth
making noises at each other
in sequences, laughing too.
She kicks and waves her arms,
I see her joy in such minuscule achievements.

When I hold her, I am adding
momentarily to the maternal circle,
so imperative around mother and baby
in these early weeks of life.
That love, a new consciousness
from the distance of years, gathers
more perspective within its blanket.
And the spaces and gaps
in time and years
allow the feelings and memories
of those early days of my motherhood
to arrive in focus for a second time.
But differently.

The sharp slither of remembrance of those
disorientating months as long
as thirty years ago, composes part of
the resonance of the maternal shield,
my more long-lived, presence
in the links of our chain.

# *B a b y s i t t i n g*

I am not dressed like a granny,
I can squeeze into an updated version.
Baby-boomer jeans are a forgiving uniform
and I don't have the emoji's brown bun;
though I do have the glasses.

I offer them some hours of freedom.
Sitting alone on their settee,
I hear a television floors above,
in the running down of a gentle evening.

In no time at all
the baby monitor flickers.
I hold my breath;
her disjointed cry
bursts into the room.

In the gloom she is restless,
she's lost her dummy.
I stroke her head as instructed.
Her eyes flash open.
She's registered the different touch.

Instantly, I absorb this as failure
which brings memories
of my own crossing
the frontiers of motherhood;
how awed I was by the compulsion
of that fierce protectiveness.
Now I feel the familiar
maternal burning in me -
recalling how discomforting it was,
so wild and confusing,
as my baby and I edged
awkwardly into our new life.

And now, my daughter's baby
Is squirming and wriggling;
Her crying escalates,
feeding itself, as if
the sound of her desperation
terrifies her, too loud in her ears.
She breaks into a dreadful crescendo
of trembling misery,
until she's kicking,
sobbing. Howling.

I hold her, clasp her tight,
whispering softly, hoping my voice
threads into her brain, to soothe,
cut through her distress,
but in the tension of
her arched back, flailing limbs
she is fighting to be free of me,
to leap from my arms
without knowing where she is going.
I can scarcely contain the force of her energy,
her will to be free of me.

I am aware of how old my body is
against her fresh new strength.
Flexible as a young tree.

I want to protect her,
comfort her, rescue her from
her primal horror of losing her mother.

But I'm the wrong person.

Wrong arms.

Wrong smell.

Wrong voice.

I am the wrong person.

## *Sleep's Healing*

In the morning,
the sun breaks through the edge of the curtains.
She lies swaddled in her cot,
wrapped tightly in a blanket;
sobs, breathy gulps finally pacified
in the nest of her mother's arms,
safe enough to relax into the void of night.

So young, living in senses, feelings;
she knows in her being,
the shield of her mother's body,
the comfort of her smell,
the peace of her soothing voice,
over and over again,
as light follows dark,
satiation follows hunger.

Many nights and many days,
many sleeps build repetitive rhythms
which create her existence.

Her mummy greets her
with a sing song, 'Hi.'
Legs kick out, arms wave,
a smile spreads across her face;

I peer over the side of the cot.

She beams.

## *Sunrise, Sunset*

Her feelings, easy as water,
flow through her limbs,
revealed in her flailing
arms and legs,
face breaking
into tremulous cries;
sudden beams of delight.

        Along the path of sixty,
        movement of limbs,
        sometimes stiff and careful
        muscles often ailing and weak;
        decades of work and worry
        have worn them down,
        flaccid elastic over-used;

No separation of body
emotions and brain to mute
the wild inflammations of need;
desperate cries; primitive, raw,
which her mother urges to decipher.

Emotions, opaque
buried in folds of years,
contorted, split, fractured, re-wired,
so that I can't find their roots,
or re-arrange them easily
to be more appropriate to the event.

No doubt, consideration
or reflection to temper
the force of emotions
that sweep through her:
no misinterpretation,
judgement from the outside
to tell her not to feel.

A harsh voice, jerky tones of irritation,
lack of explanation, a clipped order
which shrivelled the little girl,
festers deep in my bones;
clouds my perceptions.

Hers are lucid, distinct,
clear as the sun's rising
at dawn, fresh colour lifting
the landscape, dewy, plains
of lucid reflected light, gleaming
uncompromising and strong.

Will she bring me
a capacity to understand
through holding her,
cherishing her;
seeing her beginning to my end?

Her mother strokes her temples
gently, to still her sounds, her fears,
until her lashes sink on her cheek
as she breathes into her sleep.

## *Good Enough Grandmother*

She spreads glinting jewels of intensity,
offering unconditional love from the leisure of retirement.
Visceral mother love re-awakened at the grandchild's arrival.
The memory of her loneliness as a first-time mother stirs
as she watches her daughter emerge into her new role.

Feelings loom up as magma from the deep,
a longing to protect and shield mother and baby.
It surges from the subterranean shifting of generations;
the invisible weight of genes; chains which bind them.
The baby's created a new alchemy of biology,
fused with ancient instincts, embraced by social change.
Webs woven from the past, present and future
gather up to shape her for the task.

She wants so badly to get it right,
certain of the wisdom she's harvested.
There is such a desire to transmit
lessons learned from her own life,
to share her experience and convictions,
some gleaned from adulthood when she
rejected her mother's style of parenting.

But her wisdoms are uninvited;
sometimes her timing is inappropriate
borne of her regretted mistakes.
It takes a while to see that she is
a victim of social change herself.

She must step aside, for time is moving fast.
Now she needs to tune into the baby's smile.
There's a miracle she was too busy for the first time.
This is their time, not hers.
The shape of her life is fading and closing;
but it has its own momentum.
She can polish those jewels intensified
by love and age, let them shine
and just be a good enough grandmother.

## *T w o*

They gaze
at the iced teddy-bear cake
which is edged with smarties -
jewels in the snow;
light softens their faces
in the winter gloom.

Encircled in her father's arms,
she stretches her hand to her mother,
clutching her finger, keeping her close.

Family of three in November shadow,
faces bent in halo of candlelight,
eyes lowered, transfixed
by two tiny flames.

Her first two years of life.

# *Summer Baking*

We pummel pastry and toddler-talk
through the summer's afternoon.
She presses down the rolling pin
with all her strength;
scraps break from the mixture.
I compress them into a ball,
hand it to her to flatten.
Our hands make it warm and crumbly.

She chooses an elephant pastry cutter,
a cat and a dog, twisting them
into the floury mixture.

We watch them brown
through the smeared glass.
The biscuit smell spirals
into the hot kitchen,
soaking our nostrils,
stirring our taste buds.

Again and again, she asks,
'Can we eat them?'
'Let's wait until they're cooked.'
She hides her face,
curls fall around her cheeks.

'What's wrong?'
She wants to eat all
the biscuits she made
NOW.
My hand on her back;

'It's hard to wait, I know.
When they're cool,
let's choose two for you,
two for Mummy
and two for Daddy.'

When it's time, I open the door,
heat rushes up from the oven.
We wait - not too hot
for the delicate skin of her mouth.

She lifts the crooked elephant to her lips,
she crunches its leg slowly,
savouring, eyes alight;
we smile at each other
over our precious biscuits.

## *Through the French Windows*

On a long hot London day,
a toddler, in a light white cotton dress,
runs on humpy grass
which slopes down to the fence;
where the summer foliage muffles
the electric whine of a passing train.

Her brown legs,
firm, rounded,
lift and bounce upwards,
as she weaves around the shrubs;
trailing a cloud of shrieks and laughter.

She runs nowhere,
in and out,
backwards and forwards,
without intention or goal,
rapid movement of her feet;
being and feeling
the power in her body,
joy, energy, delight:

while her grandmother,

who has forgotten how to run aimlessly,

follows letting her lead,

legs aching, energy heavy,

stirred by an ancient childish memory

of running in an orchard of tall grasses.

The little girl grabs a trowel she's seen her mother use,

plunges it into the moist black earth,

gathers it up, depositing it in the cleave

of an abandoned brick,

tapping it repeatedly, enjoying its metallic sound.

Then she looks at her grandmother,

who rests in the garden chair.

Then at her mother,

through the French windows

in the cool gloom, silently

folding sheets and towels,

placing them in a pile on the table.

## *M i d s u m m e r   B a b y*

The wind howls,
whips at our hair,
coats flap and fly.
Car doors swing from our hands,
slate grey waves of the lake
skim and scud, lift and fall,
fast slicing soft ethereal
green of banks against
shadowed green forests.
Streams of light lifting liquid air;
delicate hue of satiny blue
of a Sligo mountain, lost in
a sky of visionary iridescence.

Seventy year old granny
climbs up the steps in a sheltered wood
on the hill, chickens wander, foraging
where the sun is pale,
spilling through the leaves
falling into pools
around the base of the trees.

Will she know when
the second baby is coming?
Is there a genetic thread that will tug
inside her, as breathless, she climbs
upwards to find the view.

Will she know
when the earth tilts, heaves, breaks open;
when the moon slips to the surface of the land,
flooding it with milky night; when the
marking of time speeds and collapses;
the cry of pain, panting of the heart...
Waters swamping, flooding, engulfing,
her beloved daughter exhausted...

Will she know when the delicate baby is here,
transforming a day to a memorable birthday?

# A New Life

The moon moves silently across the hours
under a cloudless summer dome,
bowing to the delicate light of dawn,
over pale stripped fields,
with their ghostly stacks of hay.
Cows sleep. Still as rocks.

Tinges of fear sharpen the horizon;
night trees emerge
from the lumpen shadows
pencilling in filigree shapes
against the chromatic backlit sky.

Will I know of my daughter's labours,
the mother's message, like an alarm
calling in the long light night?

Will the chain, which links us three
wrench at me, casting unease,
disturb me through the night
leading me to the phone,
bringing a second baby
granddaughter into our lives?

Will I feel through skin
a sign beyond the brain,
a sign in my blood
that she is here?
Will I sense her struggling
in the dark, as the sun wakes,
brings her, with the light
into her parents' home?

Changing her family's life,
adding another link to the chain.

Will I see that my daughter's
moved on and away,
as I shift back to watch
as her life plays out;
and she creates the family,
I was unable to,

as I imagine the chain's
unknown links beyond me.

## *Meeting Another Baby*

She looks up at me
from another world,
newborn, fresh, vulnerable;
an echo of me in her genes,
a generation removed,
forcing me to face my horizons.

Experience forms advice:
I find resistance.
But the sea goes on
smashing the rocks;
throws back my words,
debris sucked away,
tossed back to the shore,

impelling my wisdom away,
searching for modern meaning,
investigating, hurting:
discovering mismatch.

Until like rough, uneven stone,
I am unintentionally worked
into smaller, finer pieces,
abrasions dismantling structure,
transformed to something smoother;

the silence of hewn glass,

or a grain of sand

tightened, completed,
to be more understanding perhaps?

A whole world to begin again.

# *My Daughter, (Who Made This Possible)*

Her father and I
dreamed that we would
give her all we did not have,
so grand were our ideals.
We were pioneers breaking
the rules of decades.
Youthful ignorance
reaching to the unknown.

When I was pregnant,
we spent afternoons together
she and I,
in the Autumn
listening to Mozart.
I watched the tree,
silhouetted through condensation
against twilight winter.

She had a stillness
when she was born;
she observed me from
another world,
staring at me
with her dark
metallic eyes.

That night together
behind the curtains,
surrounded by howling babies,
I fell from a high place
into her breathing
milky smell, our milky smell,
resting my cheek on
her silky temples
where the soft beauty
of her life was
all around me like music.

But all those earlier years
which formed us, her parents,
social shifts, the timing
of our unreal expectations,
could not be spirited away,
or pushed behind us.
And isolated, I lost myself. And him.

Now she is the middle link of our
chain of women,
drying the tears of her daughters,
healing jealousies,
hanging their clothes fresh in the sun,
planting their food in the London soil;
leaving at 7 am to catch the train to work,
back by 3:15 to be there, waiting,
after their school day as they carry
their bags of books,
loosened ties, tousled hair.

As it was for me,
I see her years ahead, chasing time,
beyond my span of life,
when I am no longer here.
If she reaches a time of reflection,
I will be an absent presence.

And I know so little of the unconscious legacy
I may have left in her as a young child.
My distress at her father's leaving,
the pull of a family home for her;
the undertow I carried from my parents
which they would never have known.

I have found no truths, but shapes,
ghosts of suggestions, possibilities;
in my search to understand -
I do not know what is genetic,
what is social, how circumstance
describes our destinies. So much is an
unconscious alchemy, with its invisible
subterranean life moving silently through
the links of our chain.

Though I do know it was she
who made all this possible.

## *R e p a r a t i o n*

Being a mother is altered forever
when a husband goes;
the early life of a family dissolves,
though there still remains
a faint image of the three of us at the birth.

Then two households co-existed.
One with a mother, daughter and two cats.
Another family was created around my daughter,
four children; half/step siblings
now a bulwark and support for her.

When my baby carried her babies.
time ceased to be linear.
Memories of holding my newborn
ran parallel as I held my granddaughters.
Her birth drifted up to the present
sitting alongside her babies' births.

All through,
invisible tectonic plates of feeling
transmuted, re-arranging,
sometimes causing disarray,
like the passage of adolescence,
or the transition to motherhood.
I began with one identity at that phone call,
'I'm pregnant Mum,'
and emerged with another.

Could being a grandmother offer a plateau for reflection?
Employment finished. The last parent gone.
My role as a daughter concluded.
Would there be a search for a new meaning?
Redemption? Reparation?

Could it come from the afternoon hours
alone with each granddaughter?
An unearthing of the laughing mother I might have been?
A different unknown mother inside me?

The excitement of the first granddaughter's steps:
She staggered down the hallway,
lurching, arms like sails guiding her,
falling into her mother's delighted cries.

She with her dark curls, toddled in her mother's shoes,
heels scraping on the kitchen floor,
wearing a strange ensemble
of a baby grow, carrying a gigantic handbag.

When the second girl was born, she burrowed in
her mother's arms - my daughter exhausted, sat in
a darkened room, the curtains shutting out
the brightness of the summer light,

while upstairs the elder granddaughter embraced me
into the theatre of her fantasy games.
I played husband, doctor, nurse, school friend.
As the sun moved across the sky,
I re-entered the magical days of childhood,
away from reality, living within the precious
stories of her invention, her psychic world.

The younger daughter grew older,
tottered unsteadily in the garden,
her family surrounded her, calling encouraging words,
until she fell right into her sister's arms.
Both collapsed into a laughing heap on the grass.

In the afternoon, she sat on the bottom stair
in a sunbeam, her blonde hair falling
around her shoulders, intent, concentrating;
arranging objects beside each other
mysteriously enacting a secret pattern.

I am not their mother. I cannot re-live what has passed.
But I am still a mother. I know that in spite of the
visceral joy of being that grandmother, my mothering continues
forever.

When I visit, I am embraced inside the family,
I have had gifts of days alone with each granddaughter -
long present moments reminding how hard being a mother can be,
shut off from the outside world, time moving so differently with a
child.

I travel to see them, putting my energy into tired limbs,
love firing aching muscles; playing ball, hide and seek,
grandmother's footsteps; pig-in-the-middle;
their cries in a London garden echoing in long summer evenings.
I capture myself as a child in their games and laughter,
then collapse exhausted and satisfied at home.

My trips to London have placed me in their hearts;
I am Grandma. So maybe those lost years of motherhood,
when I was unable to create the family I longed for,
there has been redemption. Reparation

in the joy of seeing my daughter, the mother I could not be,
encircled in her family, sharing with her husband,
her place certain; coloured cards of love from her daughters
on the mantelpiece, as the family of four sit at the table
in the sun drenched kitchen, for their evening meal.

## *Before I Go*

Life beyond my eyes
mists and rolls on inevitably.
What joins us is the mystery of
genes and inheritance.

She will see me in herself
and wish the opposite,
as she forges her own path.
What is left of me will
meld into her and her children
stirred in with their difference.

My uniqueness will dim
with each grandchild,
the sadness of my lost
motherhood will fade
to acceptance.

With age comes
delight in the children's
open lucidity, their fresh eyes;
while fearing the trends for their future,
about which I can do nothing.

Now I am to flow
into the ancestral sea
so death will not matter.
All will continue without me,
my special version of life
will eventually die,
and be a distant memory,
or a fleeting thought;
A story told.

## *The  Chain*

The women stand,
translucent ghosts reaching
back into history,
each joined by a mystery
lying beneath understanding.

Some whisper and
slip away from memory:
some remain in photos,
pale faced and still;
or given life in pages of an album,
through the gaze of a descendant.

Others leave their voices
to echo inside their daughters,
obeying maternal precepts or
choosing their own thoughts;
filtering genetic osmosis unknowingly,
repeating familial patterns and professions.

A phantom feature captures light
on the face of a grandchild,
the gift of momentary illumination ,
recognition gives a brief frame of existence;
then vanishes, as another different and similar,
dances to her tune, or rails against fate.

The chain opens and closes,
each link joined by invisible twine,
reaching on to a future
where each life weeps and speaks,
breathing in and out: in and out;
bringing birth, joy, loss, death.
Figures of mothers fade,
drift away and become
shadows of remembrance.

# *Author Thanks*

VALERIE WISHES TO ACKNOWLEDGE THE invaluable support of the following:

For the cover illustration: Paul Wrigley.

For editing, proof reading, support and feedback:

Meriel Wrigley, Gill Dunstan and Wendy Vacani.

For technological, presentation and moral support: Paul Little.

For support, listening and encouragement: Ada Mournian, Elizabeth Taylor, Richard Taylor, Carrie Jaffe, Annie Saunter, Imogen Lloyd and Peter Back.

Valerie would like to acknowledge years of support, feedback and friendship from Culm Valley Writers. Special thanks go to Sophia Roberts who was there at the very beginning before the group was properly formed.

Finally, gratitude and thanks go to the members of the Solitary Writers, (in particular to Peter Blaker for his encouragement) and to the group for their warm understanding and support.

VALERIE TAYLOR GREW UP IN Buckinghamshire, lived in London for over 20 years, (where. she attended writing classes at the City Lit), and has lived in Devon for nearly 20 years.

She has written stories, poetry and journals since childhood – publishing two poems in the '70s. During this time she also wrote a novel and there is an unfinished journal on being pregnant, both of which will probably remain in the drawer!

Valerie has one daughter who lives with her family in London.

Valerie taught in infant and junior schools, Adult Literacy and latterly assessed and supported students with dyslexia. During this time while working and being a single parent, she gave up writing.

After retirement, on moving to Devon, Valerie took up writing again and joined the Culm Valley Writers which has been meeting now for over 10 years. The group has recently self – published a booklet on the pandemic called *'Viral Verses'*. Two members of the group have already self-published poetry books.

Valerie recently joined another group called Solitary Writers and has read poems on local radio.

This is her first book of poems which has been 12 years in the making.

# *Reviews*

*'A beautifully written collection of poems that will speak to every woman, whether daughter, mother or grandmother. The author takes you on an emotional journey, capturing with great honesty the conflicting emotions, fear and joy and wonder of becoming a grandmother.*

*A wonderful gift for anyone about to become a grandmother.'*

*Meriel Wrigley*

*'A beautifully written personal journey of reflection and discovery, underpinned by the powerful maternal bond. The overarching theme for me is that this poetic narrative is essentially a love story.'*

*Imogen Lloyd*